Copyright © 2023 Barbara Soehner
All rights reserved. No part of this book may be used or reproduced in any manner without the written permission of the copyright owner except for the use of quotations in a book review.
First paperback edition July 2023
Editing by Valerie Lorraine Productions
Photo credits; Barbara Soehner

All rights reserved.
ISBN: 9798856039862

Well, hello Mr. Cancer

A collection of poetry
and messages to friends
By Barbara Soehner

From the author of
The Glittering Bird REBORN

THE GLITTERING BIRD REBORN

@BARBARA_SOEHNER

BARBARA SOEHNER

Dedication To The Special Men In My Life

My Son, Christopher
May he always remember my love

My Brother, John
He has a heart of gold

My Therapist, Mark
Thank you for your belief in me

ACKNOWLEDGEMENTS

I would like to express my thanks to all the beautiful people who have supported me during this difficult journey. The community of Instagram has held me in their arms and poured out their love to my frightened soul. Thank you to Valerie BeingyouBeingtrue @poetrysupportbybt who arranged many poetry marathons that raised money for my Go Fund Me. This helped so much with expenses not covered by my insurance. So many poets contributed their time and read their wonderful poems with passion.

To my dear friends, Lavinia Alberi Auber - My Angel Friend, Janaya Stephens, Daniel White, Bryan Edwards, Mike Dennis, Sukhman Sidhu, Emily Langford the beautiful friend, who first put Well Hello, Mr. Cancer into my reality, Ismet, Ruchka, Donald, Robert A. Cozzi. Joe Steele, Arsenio, Angela Psalm, SueAnn Summers, Kaori Fuji, Brian Stout.

To my Editor and friend Valerie Lorraine, thank you for your endless love, patience and beautiful encouragement 🎩❤️

My Oncologists Dr. Teresa Shao, Dr. Manjeet Chadha, my surgeons Dr. Konstantin Zakashansky and Dr. Gennadiy Grigoryan and beautiful Erika, the nurse who administered all my chemotherapy with the kindness of an angel.

So many people were good to me and I can't possibly name them all, I am blessed and grateful. Thank you from the bottom of my heart.

Content

Mr. Cancer — Page 1

I Might Die — Page 5

Waiting — Page 7

Angel In My Mind — Page 12

There Has To Be Away — Page 13

My Mind — Page 15

My Creativity — Page 20

Sad Today — Page 26

I Don't Know What To Do — Page 28

Comfortably Numb — Page 37

Content

Love	Page 41
It's Okay	Page 45
Abaracadabra	Page 52
When Hope Dies	Page 57
Hard Day	Page 61
I Will Hold You When You Cry	Page 64
Joy	Page 67
Peaceful Land	Page 70
Forever	Page 72

Content

Folded Soul	Page 77
Just A Little Kind	Page 81
Wandering Alone	Page 84
Just Give Me Time	Page 86
Special Friends	Page 89
Three Friends	Page 90
Sweet Nectar	Page 93
I Wish I Could Cry	Page 99
Will I Ever Have That Again	Page 104

Content

What's It Like In Heaven	Page 109
Shithead Cancer	Page 111
My Legs	Page 114
Pain	Page 120
Who Are You	Page 124
Relax	Page 129
Where Did Joy Go	Page 133
Empty Words	Page 135
Flawed	Page 139

Content

I Am Very Fragile Now — Page 143

Do We Belong Together — Page 146

Friends Of Mine — Page 149

My Truth — Page 151

Thoughts — Page 153

My Hair — Page 155

Kind Love — Page 158

Barbara Soehner

MR. CANCER

Well how do you do
MR. CANCER

I am sorry to INFORM YOU

I am not happy to make your

ACQUAINTANCE

as a matter of fact
I was startled and shocked
when I found out you were
living in my body

You're a pretty sneaky
individual
I never knew you were there
until I started to bleed
then I went to see what was
going on

Well Hello, Mr. Cancer

This past Tuesday, I went to the hospital
and I had a surgery and they found you
They took many pictures and waited for the results
Yesterday I got a call from the doctor's office
They said "Please come down to the office"
It was then that I knew it was you MR. CANCER
If it hadn't been you the doctor just would've said 'Oh everything's OK'
So here I am now MR. CANCER dealing with you
This Monday, I will go for cat scans
to see if you've spread to other parts of my body

Barbara Soehner

I will BEAT you MR. CANCER
I have so many loving friends
in this community
and they are just pouring out
BEAUTIFUL love from
EVERYWHERE
It really helps me to feel
strong.
I'm scared.
But I will BEAT you.

Well Hello, Mr. Cancer

Barbara Soehner

I Might Die

I think today is the hardest day
I've had to face in my life
Yesterday I was told the stage of my cancer
STAGE 3
I will need radiation and chemotherapy
On March 16 the journey will begin
It is the beginning of chemotherapy
Then followed by five days radiation
For five weeks
Followed by another day of chemotherapy
A two week rest, and then months more of chemotherapy

Well Hello, Mr. Cancer

What's the point I asked myself
To put myself through all of this?
Well if I don't do it
There's a pretty good chance
I will die within the next few years
So I decided to go ahead with it
I'm really scared
Really, really scared
I'm paralyzed just laying in my bed now
I just don't wanna get up, it's really hard

I am paralyzed today
Can't do a thing but stare at the ceiling
Filled with fear

Barbara Soehner

WAITING

Is there anything more uncomfortable than waiting
Waiting...such a helpless condition
We are all so trusting in this world
Really kind of helpless when it comes to our health
When someone else is in control
Surgeons are gifted and talented
They save lives
When it comes to removing rubbish from your body
Rubbish that suddenly appeared without warning
In my case, it was scary to be cut open
Have things removed from my body, from my soul

Well Hello, Mr. Cancer

My uterus has been thrown away
There is an empty space inside me now
Empty inside
As a woman I want to know
What's going to happen next
Did the cancer disseminate
What stage is it in
There were two surgeons…one removed my lymph nodes
The other my uterus
Apparently the lymph nodes hold the clues
There is no immediate answer
I've been told "you will have to wait till next week to see the doctor"
Another seven days of not knowing where I am

Barbara Soehner

Nothing I can do
Yeah...waiting is really, really hard
I'm not happy about it at all
Waiting has taken my hope
Made me scared...scared because

I don't know
What the answer will be

Well Hello, Mr. Cancer

Barbara Soehner

Dear Friends

Hi friends. I'm scared. Feb 9th is the surgery. Please keep me in your prayers. This little poem popped out today and was a great comfort. Love you all so much. Thank you with all my heart for your beautiful support

THE ANGEL IN MY MIND

The angel in my mind
quiets my pain
he spreads his wings
and pushes my grief away
so much to cope with
Life can be so unkind
so I call out for help
to the angel in my mind

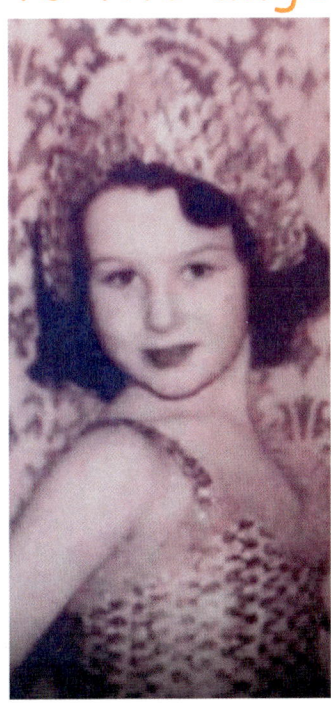

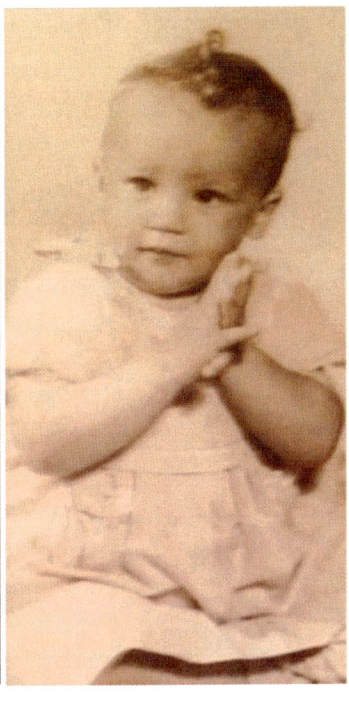

Barbara Soehner

There Has To Be A Way

My knees are crying
My stomach dying
Slowly inside I am
crumbling
This stronger chemo is a
Mean cruel monster
Three more sessions to
go
Damn this is hard
My ears are shooting
Bullets in my brain
Ripping my thoughts
I scream 'Stop
Please stop!'
I am brave and so
I'll go on but I won't lie
It's bad….so bad

Well Hello, Mr. Cancer

Again and again I ask
'Why me?'
So alone and afraid
Like a broken glass vase
I fell to the floor and shattered
There has to be a way
To pick myself up
There has to be a way

Barbara Soehner

My Mind

Part of my mind is frozen like
a piece of ice
It won't melt, it's just stays in
one place
unable to thaw
Part of my mind is frightened
there doesn't seem to be a way
out of this pain
I don't like it at all, it's cruel
Part of my mind is confused
because I don't know why this
is happening to me

I used to be so carefree, so
free
Yes part of my mind is frozen
unable to move

Well Hello, Mr. Cancer

unable to smile, unable to sing
Unable to be anything
BUT A LUMP OF PAIN

Part of my mind has forgotten
How to walk
I hide in my bed day after day
Night after night
Safe and alone from this
Awful plight

Part of my mind adores sleep
I journey with the angels
They carry me far away
To a magic land of peace

Barbara Soehner

Part of my mind begs them
To let me stay
I always come back to face yet another day
Okay mind, I'll make you a deal
I will get up on my pins and needles legs. I won't give up,
I promise.
Today I may even smile

Well Hello, Mr. Cancer

Barbara Soehner

My Creativity

My creativity is frozen
For I feel so helpless
Cancer really sucks
I ask myself over and
over again
Why did this happen to me
Why, why, why
My creativity is frozen
It won't budge
Did I flee into space?
Can I be rescued?
Will I survive ?
Damn today is a scary day
To be alive

Barbara Soehner

My creativity is frozen
It was always my best friend
Now it's run away
It's terrified of what
May be the end

My creativity, please thaw out
Don't leave me now
I need you
I need your strength
Your hope
Your belief things
Will go right

Well Hello, Mr. Cancer

I need you
Please blossom like
A beautiful tulip
Smile at me
Hold me close
You are my joy

Please, my Creativity
This is my wish
Take away my doubt
Help me soar again to
The magic place
Where my soul takes pride
In my gift with words
In my joy for life

Barbara Soehner

Dear Friends

Here it is another day and it is harder than yesterday. Just found out an elderly aunt is dying. So much death these last few years. I am so grateful to everyone in this community of poets. You are a beautiful, loving, calming family. Thank you for that. I posted on Instagram from happier days with my son. He was such a joy. The flowers are a beautiful gift he sent me on my birthday.
Even though we are not in touch, he always reaches out on my birthday. Only time will tell what this year will bring

Beautiful flowers and elephant
   sent to me from my son

Barbara Soehner

Dear Friends

Hi everyone. I am completely blown away by all the magical love. So grateful for the 12 hour marathon planned for this Monday to raise funds for my cancer treatments starts on May 3rd. A glorious way to start my birthday week as I will be 76 on May 5th. Ha ha I think once you pass 75 you are officially in the elder club. Thank you to all my beautiful family for your love and support. I wrote the poem below on Sunday. I was sad but it's okay, sadness happens. It's life !!!

Sad Today

Sad today but it's OK
some days I just can't
make it out of the dark
the dark such a powerful place
It's hard when you're left out again
which is what I feel today

Sad today
I guess I have a good reason to be sad
I wish I'd hear from my son
every day it gets harder and
every day it seems more real
that I never will

Barbara Soehner

Sad today one more radiation
to go
I should be happy
but then the old chemo kicks
in and
Its gonna be a rough game
so I will once again say
I'm sad today

I Don't Know What to Do

I don't know what to do, I don't like this pain
this physical pain it's just the worst
It's there all the time now
I don't know what to do
It won't leave me be, and it's taking up my brain, and all of my thoughts
I'm just not free to be anymore
I'm not free to be me
I don't know what to do, my creativity got lost in a box somewhere
I can't remember where
I put the box on a shelf filled with clutter

Barbara Soehner

it is somewhere in the garbage
I can't find it
I can't find my creativity
All I am doing is being
absorbed by pain
I don't like this feeling
I don't know what to do
Where are the beautiful
rainbows and flowers, and
glorious colours that always
were in my brain giving me
some pretty ideas, and things
I cherished and loved
Where are they now?
All I see now are boring empty
complaints

Well Hello, Mr. Cancer

I don't know what to do
I know
I can dig through all my
notebooks
filled with poems I've written
Maybe I'll find some happy
times
they were there I'm sure of
that
Although right now it doesn't
seem possible
So much of my life has gone
by, it's true
I'm older now can't turn back
the clock just have to keep
going ahead
Alone and scared
I don't know, I don't know
I don't know what to do

Barbara Soehner

Well Hello, Mr. Cancer

Dear Friends

Don't ask me why, it's just that I love
my radiation machine.
It's my friend, it reminds me of R2D2.
You remember the sweet little robot in Star Wars?
Well anyway something about it, I don't know it really looks so similar.
I feel safe underneath it.
I feel like it's helping me get better.

Barbara Soehner

Yesterday the little machine broke and
so many people were waiting for their radiation.
I waited over two hours and then they put me in another machine,
an old machine.
I was very sad
because it wasn't R2-D2.
But, I knew it was helping me,
Anyway it scared me. It shook and made a noise
R2-D2 never makes a noise.
He's back again today and I am so happy to say I love you R2-D2!
Stay that way, be my friend always till this nightmare of cancer goes away.

Well Hello, Mr. Cancer

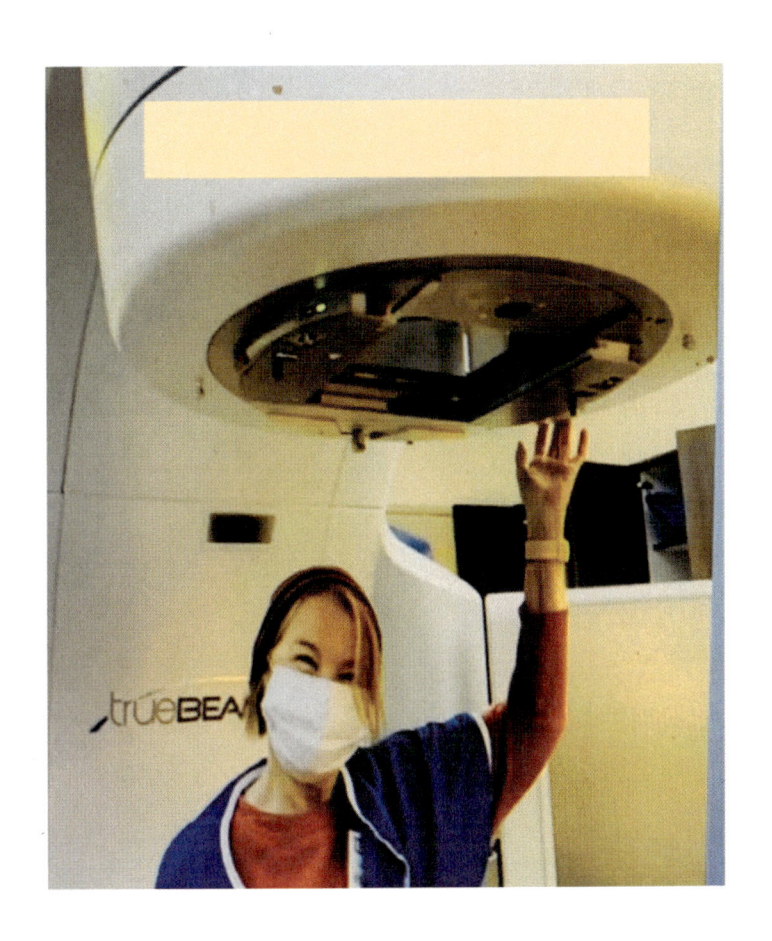

Barbara Soehner

Dear Friends

Goodbye R2D2. I never said goodbye last week. Now it's been one week since my last radiation treatment and I am actually starting to feel human. I am so grateful to all of you for the love you have sheltered me with. Excited about the Marathon coming up this Monday. It is really amazing and I thank you from the bottom of my heart. The picture you see here is of the simulation of my pelvis which they used to protect my bowel and bladder during the treatments.

Well Hello, Mr. Cancer

Barbara Soehner

Hi everyone. This is in response to a prompt by @antipoetic.revolution, Comfortably Numb. Some days I sit stuck unable to move. Hours go by and I feel numb far away from myself.

Comfortably Numb

Numb
What is it
I don't know...can't feel it
Numb
Who are you
Are you me
Afraid and dead
Inside

Well Hello, Mr. Cancer

No that's not me
Numb came to visit
Long ago
To protect my smile

Always sad I was
So I found a place
To stay safe as
No one could reach me
I had a new face

It's not so bad being alone
On your own can be powerful
You are the boss
Hooray a relief
No busy bodies poking in
Their pathetic feed

Barbara Soehner

Numb
What is it
I don't know...can't feel it
Numb
Who are you
Are you me
No I'm a friend
A way to mend
A broken heart

Okay numb
I hear you
I like this place
Being comfortably numb

Well Hello, Mr. Cancer

Barbara Soehner

LOVE

Love is the secret
Love is the answer
When everything falls down and
Collapses...goes into a deep ravine
You think there's no way to get out
Love brings you out

Love is magic, love is a gift
Who knows where it comes from
It's been a rough, rough week and
Just like that my brother showed up
Showered me with love and now
I'm like a new person

Well Hello, Mr. Cancer

Last night when I went onto the live with Danny.
Everyone showered me with so much love
Once again everything blossomed
Shined with graceful beautiful moments I will cherish forever
Thank you all so much for your love

An interesting fact love is free
Truthfully where can you find
Something so beautiful that is free
It doesn't exist
There are no boundaries to love
There are no rules to love

Barbara Soehner

It is, and you can choose to live it
Embrace it and cherish this gift
It is real and IT IS there for anyone
To grab a hold of
So go follow the yellow climbing
Staircase to the stars
The home of love
Love the open door to happiness

Well Hello, Mr. Cancer

Barbara Soehner

IT'S OKAY

It's okay not to be okay
Don't have to smile and fake your pain
It is what is
Just be, that's all, just be
People all around telling you this, telling you
"Chill out, let it go, be positive, blah blah blah"
Why pretend and push away
What is, for it is
So go where it takes you
It needs to be heard
Inside your heart there is a story

Well Hello, Mr. Cancer

Thrashing, screaming, for it
needs to get out
it is stifling you, stopping
you, you can't breathe
You're scared, WAIT damn
JUST LISTEN
IT'S OKAY NOT TO BE OKAY

Barbara Soehner

Dear Friends

Okay today is a wee bit hard but I am hanging on strong. What is …IS

Thank you again everyone for all your beautiful love.

Well Hello, Mr. Cancer

Dear Friends

Well, hi my lovely friends. Been a rough couple of days with the bone pain. I'm thrilled to say I saw the surgeon yesterday. He said he is pleased with the healing. I will have the port placed next Friday and then three more chemotherapy treatments. Looks like I will be finished in August. They will do a complete bone scan and hopefully all will be well. It is the way it is. Just will never give up. Thank you to Everyone for your support.

Barbara Soehner

My beautiful family at Bybtpoetrysupport. Barbarathon is doing another fundraiser next Thursday June 3rd. Friday I will have the Port Placement. So wish me luck. I wrote this new poem today after another disappointment. It's okay, for I will March ahead

Well Hello, Mr. Cancer

My Dad & I

My Son & I

Barbara Soehner

December 2018, Happy in Cuba

Well Hello, Mr. Cancer

Abracadabra

Abracadabra I cannot sleep
my heart is laying in a great
big heap
once again a promise was
broken
once again I feel like a token
the kind you used to slip into
the turn style
to catch the train
just a simple mechanical act

My brain is very confused,
very hurt so I guess I'm angry
too because I feel abused

Barbara Soehner

I had such hope this time would be
A golden journey for you and me
You, such an amazing free spirit
Halfway around the world
And yet once again for some reason
We failed

I am truly ready to say goodbye
No one likes a whining cry
Bravery is my middle name
Someday, I will see you again

Well Hello, Mr. Cancer

Dear Friends

Just wrote this yesterday. Sorry to be down but sometimes you just have to face the truth and walk through. I love all of you for your love and support.
I am up and awake after a very hard day of treatment. Thankfully, I had Danny's new book with me,
"Works of Friction"
The cooling cap had no room for my glasses but just knowing it was there made me smile. It is a beautiful book by a talented and beautiful soul. Just wanted to fill everyone in on what's been occurring in my treatment.

Barbara Soehner

I wore the Dignicap which is $2000, but Mount Sinai offers it for free through a grant they have. The nurse was wonderful, and carefully hooked me up. It was super cold for the first 30 minutes, but after a while you get used to being freezing cold. I will definitely continue using it for the next sessions. There will be three more over the next coming weeks. Then hopefully after the scan they will find I am healthy. Won't that be amazing? I decided to get the port after the chemo leaked and swelled the vein in my hand.

Well Hello, Mr. Cancer

The first two chemotherapy treatments were more gentle. The next four not so but God and all you beautiful family members give me so much strength.

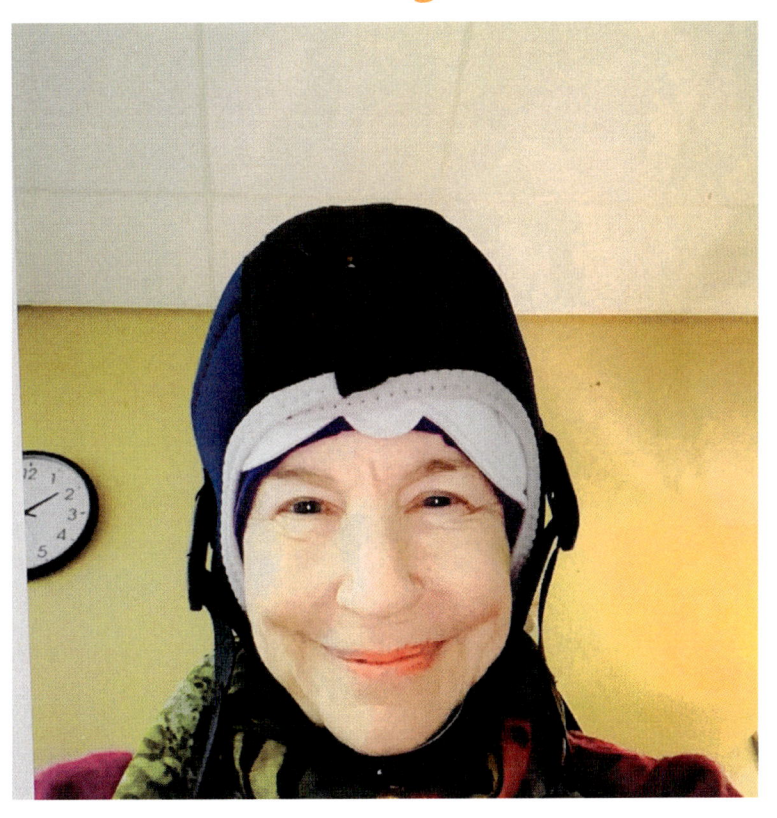

Barbara Soehner

WHEN HOPE DIES

When HOPE dies
Clouds stumble from the sky
Filled with rain
Filled with tears of pain

When hope dies courage falls
away
Nothing is okay
Nothing stays right
When HOPE dies

There is no light
Promises that should have
Been kept
GO AWAY

Well Hello, Mr. Cancer

Lies tumble down
Fill your heart with despair
There is no hope

When HOPE DIES

Barbara Soehner

Dear Friends

Hi everyone. As you can see I am tumbling down to sadness today. On June 3rd, the 12 hour Barbarthon was held on Instagram. It was magical and such a wonderful success. I thank everyone from the bottom of my heart. So, so grateful for all of you. The port placement was yesterday and damn it feels really sore. Thank God I had general anaesthesia. I was told to keep the clear bandages on for three days and not to get them wet. Then hopefully the port will be ready for the Chemotherapy on June 8th.

Well Hello, Mr. Cancer

As you can see from my poem below, I'm not feeling good emotionally but hopefully this will pass.
Love you all so much

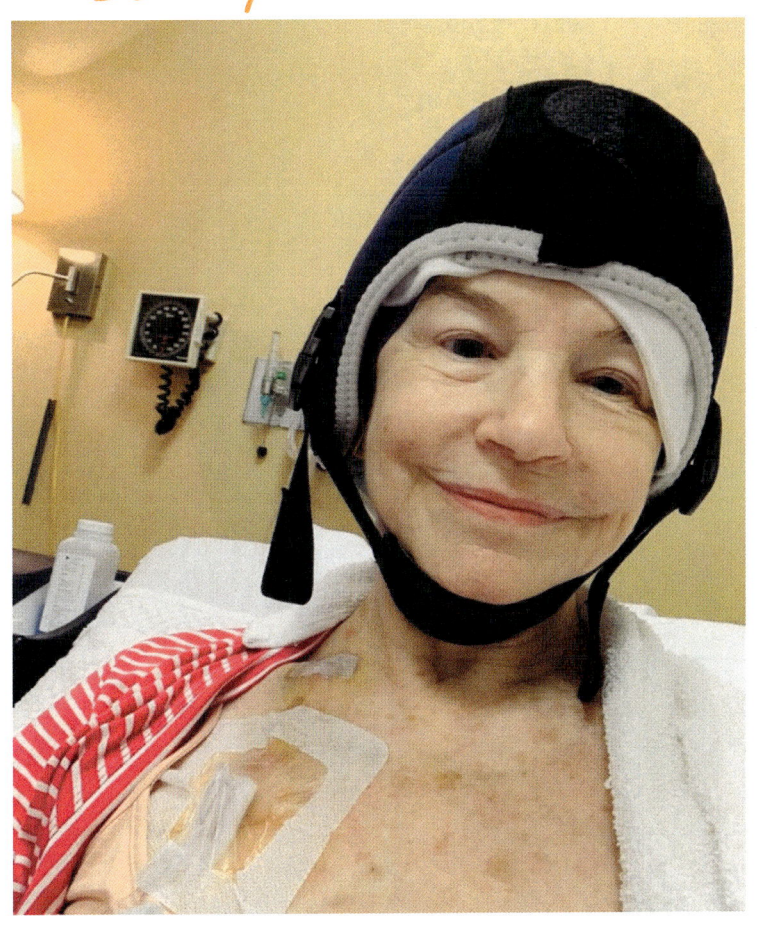

Barbara Soehner

Hard Day

I am tumbling down
To sadness
This time it's getting harder
and harder
Yesterday I touched my hair
It came out in droves
Yesterday I had the port put
in
It's so painful today
Yes this time is getting
harder and harder
in every way
On June 8th I have my 4th
chemo
It's the mean one and still
deciding
Should I wear the cooling cap
As I said my hair is falling
out in bunches

Well Hello, Mr. Cancer

Silky fine hair flying in the air
I touch my scalp and it clings
to my hand
Saying goodbye, so very sad
Today is a hard day
I ask myself why me

There is no answer
Life is life
I still pray for success
Mr. Cancer, I won't
let you win

Barbara Soehner

Dear Friends

Hi everyone. Feeling a tiny bit better. Yay, my knees stopped hurting today. I am taking it day by day and again, I am so grateful for your love and support. Here's a fun poem I wrote today.

Well Hello, Mr. Cancer

I Will Hold You When You Cry

Oh the moon, the moon
Such a strong force in our lives
Sometimes I wonder
Who is there for you?
Are you alone Mr. moon?
Do you need a hug?

No I don't think so
You've guided so many people
For so many years
For eternity you've been there
Sweet moon
I just want you to know that I love you
I love looking up at you
I love feeling your light on my face
When you're full

Barbara Soehner

I love the fact that I can count on you
For you will never go away
You are always there
You will always stay
If you are ever sad
I will pick you out of the Sky
I will hold you when you cry
Yes, sweet moon
I give you a big hug
I thank you so much for your love

Well Hello, Mr. Cancer

Dear Friends

Hi my dear, dear family of friends. I can hardly believe I had a deep long sleep. 'Happy Hope' is a great sleeping pill. I am scared shitless, but happy I had the port placed. It was the best choice. Thank you everyone for your kindness and support. This poem fell out after I heard from my son. He said he will be in touch, and that my friends, was my JOY.

Barbara Soehner

JOY

Joy is when your broken heart
Is tenderly picked up
Sunshine peeks in the window
A new journey begins

Fear and doubts fall into
A river and ripples wash away
The longings which have
Finally been answered
So much to look forward to
I pinch myself and smile at the
Joy that is ahead
My son has found a beautiful
love
She has a smile that shines
from within
The sun will shine brighter
today

Well Hello, Mr. Cancer

A long time coming plodding through
So much doubt
Flowers surround my heart
So much joy

Barbara Soehner

This is a beautiful picture I took while visiting Caserta Castle with my son years ago. I thought it perfect to post with this positive peace

PEACEFUL LAND

GOD you are so kind
You come to my mind
Without warning and ease my doubts
Such a new world is evolving
I see more, I hear more
My thoughts flow freely so
I just let them be
This secret mystery of
Where they are from indeed
It puzzles me
No need to hurry, to understand
No need to worry
This is a peaceful land

Barbara Soehner

Dear Friends

Hi friends, I'm feeling okay today. Only one more chemo to go and I am praying the scan after that will be cancer free.

Well Hello, Mr. Cancer

FOREVER

It matters to know I was loved
I am still loved
Separation and loss are painful
Sometimes things just never
go back
To the way they were
I must remind myself I was
loved
Life gave me that wonderful
gift
My sons' love
It will be there forever
I have been through so many
valleys of pain
This past year
BUT

Barbara Soehner

I have to keep saying to myself
'You're strong you will make it!'
Oh, there are days when I say
'Just give it up, maybe you won't make it,
maybe you'll die'
BUT

You know I don't believe that
I am just too powerful to die
I have too many good friends
Too many people who love me
That are urging me to go on

Well Hello, Mr. Cancer

I'm so grateful for all of you
I really am
So, forever I will go on
I REFUSE TO QUIT
That's just the way it will be
Hey Me, can you hear me???
YOU WILL BE HERE
FOR MANY MORE YEARS

Barbara Soehner

Dear Friends

Hi friends. Having a rough day today since chemo gets a little more aggressive each time. Hopefully it will be a promising outcome.

Well Hello, Mr. Cancer

Dear Friends

I know I have to stay strong and I'm scared. I'm really scared. They put a medication on my stomach after the chemo is over. I have to keep it on for 27 hours and that helps my white blood cells in my immune system, but it also is the reason for the terrible pain. So I just have to keep the faith and pray I get through this ordeal. So grateful for everyone's support

Barbara Soehner

Folded Soul

This has been a rough time
So much loss …..

I have taken my soul and
carefully found
A comfortable safe place
A beautiful oak dresser with
deep deep drawers
Inside, I put a luxurious satin
blanket
Deep purple in color
I moved my wounded soul and
folded it gently
I whispered
"Don't you worry sweet soul,
you must rest"

Well Hello, Mr. Cancer

My soul was confused but agreed
As I gently folded my wounded soul
It smiled up at me and hugged me quietly
I felt such peace for I had cared for me

Barbara Soehner

Dear Friends

This beautiful picture was taken in a square in Florence, on a Thanksgiving trip with my son Christoper. It was magical. So, so special and that is why I am sharing the poem. My heart just demanded I pen it. Damn it hurts. Tomorrow I start week two of radiation, so I'm hoping for the best. Oh what a joy it would be to hear from that boy.

Well Hello, Mr. Cancer

Florence, Italy
Thanksgiving 2018

Barbara Soehner

Just a Little Kind

Sweetie do you remember me?
I'm confused because we used to share so much
Sweetie did you forget who I was?
I wonder why
I want to cry every time
I look at pictures from the past
I see your face, your beautiful face
Especially when you were little

Oh my gosh it hurts sweetie
Please let me know why this is going on
Because if I don't know what happened...
I can't fix it

Well Hello, Mr. Cancer

I don't think
I don't think I want to die
Without ever seeing you again
Yeah I'm sick really bad
Really bad sick, Chris
I can't believe it myself,
trying to stay brave
But it would help a lot if if
you'd just wave

Just a little bit you know
No big deal
Just say hello, that's all I
need
Just a sweet hello

Sweetie do you remember me?
Can you find it in your heart
to be kind
Please I think I deserve it
Just a little kind that's all
Just a little kind

Barbara Soehner

Dear Friends

Hi friends, hope all is well.
"Wandering Alone" was born from the prompt by @deadofnightpoetry
It's been a rough time for me so though it's not a scary poem.
Damn it is a scary time.

Well Hello, Mr. Cancer

Wandering Alone

I heard a sound
Outside so loud
What could it be?
I was scared

It screeched and hissed
Like fangs of a snake
Snakes have always terrified me
What should I do?
I asked myself
What should I do?

Should I take off?
Go down to the street
Wander Alone through the city
Will anybody notice I am gone?
I haven't been well
Perhaps no one will care

Barbara Soehner

Is it time to disappear?
Is the end indeed near?
Is it time to wander alone?

Damn it's cold outside
I forgot my coat
I was so scared
I just took off

Wandering alone
Might not be the greatest idea
Perhaps I should look for comfort
In friends I hold dear

Perhaps there's still hope
But I don't think so
The writings on the wall
I think it's time to go
To wander alone

JUST GIVE ME TIME

Why can I never accept who I am?
It's still the same as all those years ago.
Alone, unwanted, no one
I felt that way you know
I really did
Today I woke up with this thought
Why can't I accept who I am?
I feel like a body walking around with a face
I don't feel me
I am lost somewhere
I have left again for the wound
The realization of aloneness
Surely pushed me back to the then of early Childhood

Barbara Soehner

Those years ago alone,
unwanted, no one
I know, I know people say,
forget it

It's the past

But NO

The past lingers secretly
inside us and
When we grab a familiar face
It comes back
If we have not healed we fall
back
Again and again.
Why can't I accept who I am?

I will. Just give me time.

Well Hello, Mr. Cancer

Dear Friends

I feel really strong today after receiving so many loving messages of support from my post updating my cancer journey. Love you all so much. Just wrote a tiny poem about some special friends who have been with me from the very start of my journey. I truly don't think I would've stayed on Instagram if it wasn't for them. They believed in me, even when I didn't believe in me. They gave me the courage to keep writing. I thank you for that beautiful friends. Oh, how lucky we all are to have this wonderful way of touching each other

Barbara Soehner

Special Friends

It's amazing when you have
certain friends
A tiny group but they are
always there for you
You can trust them with
anything that you think
They would never harm you
They always, always give you
the right advice
They are golden presents from
the gods
Oh yes, these friends, I love
them so much
They know who they are
I know they do

So thank you sweethearts
I love you so much

Well Hello, Mr. Cancer

Three Friends

Look at that face so filled with beauty and joy
Reaching out with such a loving soul
To fill my heart with happiness
It was so wonderful today, seeing you Noah
I was so sad…when you woke, your mom was on the phone with me
In your sweet little voice you quietly said
"Hello Barbara"
It was amazing, it was just like getting a beautiful angel's arrow shooting right through my heart with love

Barbara Soehner

And beautiful Poppy,
when you read me my poem
the other day;
A poem from my book
I couldn't believe it as it was
just amazing to me that you
understood it
It is a pretty deep poem and
you just liked it
You like my writing
The truth in that is worth so
much to me, so much
You are so talented Poppy,
your writing is over the top
You are going to be a world
renowned poet someday

Well Hello, Mr. Cancer

10 years old now and look at your writing
I am so so grateful to have you both in my life
I adore your mother Sweet Emily!!
She is a gift sent straight from heaven
I am so grateful for her generous heart
it gives me so much strength

Barbara Soehner

Hi kind loving family. I am feeling better today. Hip hip HOORAY. I love this new poem that came to me today.

Sweet Nectar
(Come and get me)

When powerful passions
Evolve for a stranger
Someone you're suddenly with
Perhaps they are not real
Perhaps they are longings and wishes
For someone who has not yet arrived

Someone who has not yet arrived????
Now that is a gorgeous thought
A love I have not yet met
Wow

Well Hello, Mr. Cancer

Will he smile from eyes so kind
I will tumble upside down with delight
Will he be tall and strong and handsome?
With a gentle kind soul
Will the angels above shout hooray
When he arrives?

I am giggling inside my brain
These last two weeks have
Opened a new door for me
I am so grateful to be alive
I am so ready for love...for
It's been many many years
Since love joined me in a dance

Barbara Soehner

Passion will be mine
Like a sweet nectar
I will drink it lustfully
It will nourish my heart, my soul
Every inch of me will welcome
This dream of love

But WAIT
It's not going to be a dream
It will be REAL

I am ready
COME AND GET ME

Well Hello, Mr. Cancer

Dear Friends

Hi loving people of our magical talented writing community. I just wrote this poem today and wanted to share. I will stay brave, especially due to the loving support that pours out from everyone's heart. Below is a picture of Havana, Cuba during my visit in December 2018. It makes me happy to gaze upon it again and again

Barbara Soehner

Well Hello, Mr. Cancer

Dear Friends

Today was an amazing day. Yesterday, I am happy to say, today after a zillion hours of sleep, I am feeling good and hopeful.
Thank you so much to all you beautiful friends. I am so grateful for your well wishes. It really filled my heart with courage and joy. I wrote a short poem today.
We must all continue to love each other and have hope

Well Hello, Mr. Cancer

I WISH I COULD CRY

I WISH I COULD CRY
instead of having this thing
trapped inside my body
killing me every day
this loss this ignoring

THIS NOT KNOWING

This tall locked door

Why Why Why

WHY

I WISH I COULD CRY

My mind is in a new place
today
after a really rough 20 hours
just doing nothing but
thinking

Barbara Soehner

MY MIND TODAY

Can't even think

it's sort of in a non-place
NON EXISTENT
waiting for me to get back

BUT I CAN'T

I am trapped inside this long dark hall
There are no windows...no doors
I am trapped inside this awful place

I WISH I COULD CRY

I have felt trapped before
But never quite like this
Before there was always hope

Well Hello, Mr. Cancer

Not NOW

Today HOPE is hidden

I wish I could cry
Even tears can be mean
As they stay locked in the
frozen compartment of your
brain

Barbara Soehner

Dear Friends

Hi everyone. Hope you are all safe and ready to begin this brand new week. My words below are again sad today. I know this will pass but I allow my words from deep inside my sorrow. I give them permission to fly free and release.

Barbara Soehner

Dear Friends

So much was traveling through my mind today.
I was scared about a new project. So, I spent some time looking through older poems and came across one that made me remember the last time I was in love. 2007 was a long time ago. Ha ha hope it comes again.

Well Hello, Mr. Cancer

WILL I EVER HAVE THAT AGAIN

Will I ever have that again
That passion
That stopped my heart
That made me sink into you
Will I ever have that again

Today I feel I won't
Days have passed
I won't give in for
I mustn't call….this time is
Final and so over

My heart is floating and screaming
Hurting and dying
But no I won't call
I mustn't for this will pass
Perhaps
I will be able to begin again
Someday

Barbara Soehner

It is such a horrid feeling
Like a black, black cloud
Is capturing me
Suffocating my very breath
I feel numb and dead inside
Like I am ceasing to be

I miss you so much
But what do I miss
For you
Didn't care at least
Not the way I wanted
Not the way that would
Have brightened my life

I wonder
Do you think of me
Ever
I wonder
Do you long for me

Well Hello, Mr. Cancer

Ever
I wonder
Will I ever have that again
That passion
That stopped my heart
That made me sink into you
Will I ever have that again

Barbara Soehner

Dear Friends

It's just such a hard time right now.
I feel like a broken record.
All I do is talk about the pain.
The horrific monster never goes away.
I'm scared. Monday I go for a three month check up with my oncology radiation Doctor.
The final chemo I received was so aggressive.
That horrible platinum medicine they give me causes so much pain.
Last time they lowered the dose and it was OK for a few weeks but
then, this last week the neuropathy insisted on madly pounding its razor blades living in my feet.

Well Hello, Mr. Cancer

Now I can hardly even stand up.
I'm gonna try and attempt to go to the drugstore because I ordered some stuff from Amazon that will be in my footlocker at Rite Aid.
I ordered some socks that I can wear to ease the ongoing pain.

I love this joyous online community. It is just really great, supportive and loving. Thank you everyone. That's all for today..

Barbara Soehner

What's It Like In Heaven

Racked with pain I try to begin
again
what's the point
can't stand this pain I
hate it so so much
it's really killing me

It's really weird
writing down these words
it's almost as if
the person I was,
the person who felt OK
She has gone away now and
today a new person is here
A very sad, and angry person
but that's how I am so
I've got to let it out
don't you agree or
perhaps you don't agree with
me perhaps you're tired

Well Hello, Mr. Cancer

of hearing all my grief
oh well that's life

But wait
What's it like in Heaven
Is there glorious music playing
all the time
Will my mind rest in the peace
I find
I am not afraid perhaps a
little sad
I don't do well with being
ignored
Simply because I don't
understand why
Asking a question and never
getting an answer
It hurts
So you KNOW who you are
Please answer
We may not have much time

Barbara Soehner

SHITHEAD CANCER
(A Poetically Painful Recollection)

Today I decided to start a journal about shit head cancer, even though I only have one more chemo to go
I decided to start to write down the horror that's going on in my body. It's so hard I've really isolated myself, kept to myself, kept quiet. The only time I really come alive is when I go on a live show and I'm a co-host and read other people's poetry. It makes me happy. Damn I am miserable right now I am so, so miserable

Well Hello, Mr. Cancer

Oh I hate the pain and it's here all the time from the neuropathy. God only knows if it's going to get better after the next chemo. I'll probably get worse and then they're gonna do a scan and find out if the cancer came back.
If it doesn't come back then they'll take out the port and maybe I'll be alive again.
I don't know. So I decided today to start this journal to see where it goes.
I should've started at the beginning. I hope I become alive again. I really hope I do

Barbara Soehner

I am lying here in my bed with my legs stretched out. My legs that I think are legs but they feel like automatic machine guns. They are so painful, especially my feet.
I sadly remember when I had toes that bent and stuff. Now my toes just freeze and howl with laughter at me as they're making me suffer.

This whole thing is crazy.
I don't understand how I got here but damn I'm hating it
I'm really hating being here.
Cancer SUCKS

Well Hello, Mr. Cancer

Hi lovely family. I heard from my dear friend Danny this morning, and it inspired me to write.

My LEGS

I really miss my legs
I apologize legs
I apologize I haven't been more kind to you

I always took you for granted
I woke up and there you were
I would hop out of bed
Allowing my feet to lead the way
Now I feel knives and needles and pins paralyzing you

Barbara Soehner

I'm really sad but I have to get through this
I mean there's no other way
I have to get through so my beautiful legs can live again
Move and sway and dance to the beauty of life
Be swept in the arms
Of a glorious man, I've yet to meet
Ah yes, I'm still entitled to love you see

I always felt my mama when I looked at my feet
she was 21 when she met defeat
She flew away to heaven
Such a magnificent ballerina she was

Well Hello, Mr. Cancer

I remember I used to have so much fun alone in my home dancing around the room and feeling her presence

Oh well

I pray you come back dear legs I don't want to wind up just sitting in a chair trying desperately to get around

I want to take myself to see the world
I pray, I pray, I pray you come back to me my beautiful legs your newest pain I simply don't appreciate
Quite strange really the pop of pain today is diving into my toenails

Barbara Soehner

Uterine Cancer is the worst so they had to use the platinum chemotherapy
Don't get me wrong
I am grateful the cancer is gone

But

Oh shit, I miss my legs

Well Hello, Mr. Cancer

Dear Friends

Goodbye shithead cancer! Today I got the news. The CAT scan came up CLEAR! I can hardly believe this is real. I am so grateful to God. So many people prayed for me. God listened.
I still suffer badly from the neuropathy. Will just have to be patient. The pain will subside.
Next week I will see my oncologist. She will arrange to have the port removed and once that's done, I will be Free!
Thank you all from the bottom of my heart.
Again I will say, I am so grateful.

Barbara Soehner

Picture is of the Goddess Tara who is known for protecting those on their way to spiritual enlightenment. I believe this journey through cancer since November 2020 has indeed been my journey toward spiritual enlightenment. It has been a rough road but I MADE IT!

Pain

OK here it is today and I just wanted to fill everyone in and say I really still want you to know how much I love you and appreciate you. But, oh boy, I'm having a rough time
I don't think I can get any rougher to be honest I'm just feeling like I'm kind of dead
I have no creativity left you know
I don't have the ability to write these big flowing words like so many do I just say simple things
So I'm simply saying the following

Barbara Soehner

Today is a rough day the pain it's killing me inside
It's taking me and flying me to another place, slamming my head against a great big wall telling me 'I truly may not live'
That I'm gonna be dead soon the pain is really rough today

Not feeling my legs or my feet has terrified me
When I stand on the floor, I wonder
if it's even there
I can't eat or drink I just don't care
I toss and turn and pray for night to fall
The darkness helps me understand it all

Well Hello, Mr. Cancer

I remember glorious days and
I am thankful
They were born
But now, today, wow I am
forlorn
Alone, so alone it's not fun but
Such is life
If only the pain would fucking
chill out

It's really too much

My mind is different now it's
sort of phasing away you know
like I can't concentrate and
when I do think I only think of
pain

Barbara Soehner

I miss my mind
I miss my joy
I miss my creativity
Oh, I know it will probably come back
But right now
all I think of is the pain

Well Hello, Mr. Cancer

WHO ARE YOU

You asked
"Who are you?"

I am a long long story
Born many years ago
So, very tiny, just 2 lbs
I lived in a box
They called it an incubator
For two months tubes and warmth
Fondled my soul

You ask again
"Who are you?"

Barbara Soehner

I am a survivor, but left alone
My mama died when I was three
The floor fell out from under me
I was left unsupervised as Daddy
Worked all the time

Teenage aunties, my sweet grandparents
Nanny and Jack, lots of love but I ran free
Just did what I wanted to do...as I said
No one supervised me
I loved wondering about up to Ickle Bickles
my favorite candy store
He had penny candies and for just a few cents
I'd have a special treat

Well Hello, Mr. Cancer

I was never allowed to know
my Mom's family
I think it had something to
do
with the way she died
She was just 21
I had a sister 10 days old
She went up to the heavenly
souls

No one ever said anything
again
But I think that's why my
Mom died
Sad indeed I only knew them
till I was three

I do remember that they
were special
my life has been
just so much mystery

Barbara Soehner

You asked again
"Who are you?"
Life went on
My Dad remarried
It was tough in the beginning
So different as I said
I was a free soul and didn't do
well with rules

Had one sister and three
brothers
But honestly I will say
I have always been a loner
The little match girl peeking in
From outside
I lost me a long time ago
Just finding me now

You ask again
"Who are you?

Well Hello, Mr. Cancer

I am a miracle because
Now I'm strong and know myself
And thank the beautiful angels
Who have always been close by
I am SUPER NICE

My Mother Marie, her Mom, Dad & Grandmother. 4 ♥'s I never got to know

Barbara Soehner

Hi family. Just a few positive words popped out today.

Relax

Relax, just relax
Nothing to worry about
Just relax

I am in control
Powerful way to be
Self pity
Won't get the best
Of me

Relax just relax
Nothing to worry about
But relax

For 8 months
The mountains have
Been steep, treacherous
Slippery and empty

Well Hello, Mr. Cancer

Hope had disappeared

Today I see
A tiny speck of Sun
Enveloping me
With love

Relax, it shines
Just relax
Nothing to worry about

Just relax
A new day

Will come

I'm feeling it now
A floaty feeling
So graceful and sound

Barbara Soehner

Dear Friends

Hi friends. Well it's Monday, and today I had my three month follow up with my radiology oncologist. She looked inside and was happy with how it looked. So fingers crossed for tomorrow. Trying to remain positive. Thank you everyone for your love and support. I think it's time to put this book together, I'm digging through the poems I wrote during this horrific time.

Well Hello, Mr. Cancer

Dear Friends

Hi friends. The last two days the neuropathy pain from chemotherapy has been evil. I kind of withdrew and slept a lot. But I'm back and wrote the poem below. Just refuse to give up. Thank you beautiful people for all your support. I have a beautiful book on Amazon, 'The Glittering Bird REBORN' and would love you to check it out. My apologies to all my friends for missing their live feeds and birthdays. You are so loving and I am so grateful for your support♥

Barbara Soehner

Where Did The Joy Go

Where did my joy go
I had such hope
Once again it didn't happen
Where did my joy go
I know I have to understand that
You do things the way you do
Not to be cold
It's just the way you are

BUT IT HURTS SO BAD

I don't have much now
I'm so terribly sick from the chemo
The neuropathy is evil
I don't even know if I'll ever be OK
Once again I had such hope
To speak with you
Once again you never called

Well Hello, Mr. Cancer

I AM SO TIRED OF PAIN

So where did my joy go
What is Joy anyway
I know I've written about it before
Expressing that glorious feeling
That brings a smile deep from within
The glorious feeling that makes tears
Fall from my eyes, roll down my cheek
Then bounce into the air and vanish
Where does it go
Does it really disappear
Will I ever feel it again
I pray I will

I deserve joy and so much more

Barbara Soehner

Empty Words

My words are empty today
there's nothing left
I face a scary week
I feel like giving up
I feel what's the point
Will I die?
Will I live?
I don't know
Yes that's true
I don't know
My words are empty today
All around people are pouring
out beautiful poems
I don't know where my
beautiful poems went
my words are empty today
there's nothing left

Well Hello, Mr. Cancer

I face a scary week
Flowers and moonbeams and joy and laughter
All frozen now inside my fear
Tears fall downs searching for some hope
I never ever dreamed this place
Would be my home
I want to go backwards to where I used to be
My words are empty today
I face a scary week

Barbara Soehner

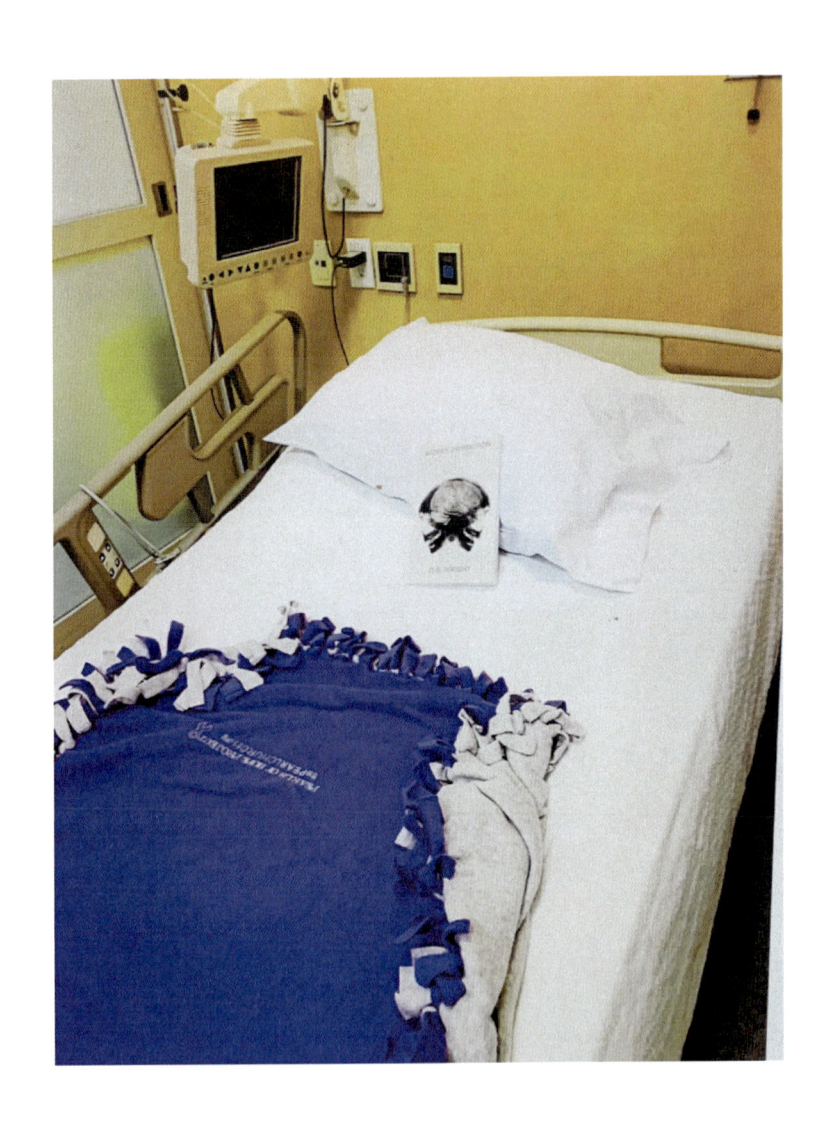

Flawed

Flawed
Where shall I begin
So many things I tried to hide
Inside out and upside down
No one ever knew
All the stuff I hid inside
No one ever knew

Flawed
A secret we can't admit
Sometimes needs to be seen
But no, no, no
What will people think
If I reveal my dreams

Growing up I was afraid
I hid inside my room
I had so much to offer
Flawed is how I zoomed

Barbara Soehner

I loved to sing but no one
Heard my sound
I was ashamed
Many years later
I found a bit of fame

Now I'm trying hard
To stay strong and brave
To live my dreams
I push away my ill found health
Try not to be afraid

Yes now I'm flawed
It's just the way it is
If I could have another chance
Live life all over again
I would give myself courage
To simply be who I am

Well Hello, Mr. Cancer

Dear Friends

I sound like a broken record. But it's true, this pain in my legs is just paralyzing me. Needles and Pins and knives all the time. My hope seems to have hidden somewhere and I am really sad. I didn't even bother to look at my messages. Then just noticed one from 9:30 this morning. It was from my son. Imagine that WOW. He said he will call tomorrow and thus the following poem evolved. Bless his heart. If he does follow through it will be a happy day. They are possible, right ?? I want to take this time to thank all of you in this beautiful community for the love and support.

Barbara Soehner

You all are the solid ground I stand on and I LOVE YOU. Please check out my book The Glittering Bird REBORN. It's on Amazon🦋 Picture is self portrait

Well Hello, Mr. Cancer

I Am Very Fragile Now

Okay
Perhaps a glimmer of magic tomorrow
Or should I say perhaps a surprise tomorrow
Careful I tell myself
Don't get your hopes up
every time you do
they are smashed and broken
I can't take it anymore
I'm too fragile now
Yes the promise of a call tomorrow
has brightened my heart today
if it doesn't come
I'll be very sad
I will understand but I'll be very sad
As I said
I am very Fragile now

Barbara Soehner

Dear Friends

Today is a really bad day. So much neuropathy in my hands and feet, I just keep going back to sleep. I haven't been outside on my beautiful street in over a week. Now I have to go to the drug store so I will venture outside. There's so many beautiful love poems here on Instagram. I feel sad because love hasn't entered the (pocket of my soul) for a very very very long time. Today I decided to post this lyric which I wrote in my sweet house in East Hampton one summer. I was separated from my ex-husband. I truly love this lyric and gave

Well Hello, Mr. Cancer

it to a wonderful musician @rubbersoulmusicjoe who put an incredible melody to it.

The picture you see here was taken on my street in Chelsea, New York City where I have lived since 1978. I hope you enjoy my lyric which was a poem before it became a song

Barbara Soehner

Do We Belong Together

You were the light of my life
We shared a space in our lives
A precious place of happy times
But then they died

We grew apart day by day
And now it might be to late
To get back where we were before
But we've got to try

I can't blame you or me
This much I know
Something keeps telling me
To just let you go

Well Hello, Mr. Cancer

We'll stay apart
We'll let our hearts decide
DO WE BELONG TOGETHER
You'll always be a friend to me
And yet
We just can't be together now

I wanna take some time, some space
I'm gonna slow down try to face
What's going on inside of me
I've got to see

I'm feeling just the way you are
This thing is tearing me apart
I'll step away and take awhile
To see if I should stay

Barbara Soehner

This is the hardest thing
I ever had to do
Hope that it turns out to be
Right for me and you

So hold me now and
Let our hearts decide
Do we belong together
You'll always be a friend to me
And yet
We just can't be together
Now

Friends of Mine

Did you ever stop to think what makes you insecure? Of course when you're not feeling well it's obvious, you're not feeling well and so everything seems dark and dismal

It can be a real, real, real drag to be insecure
It can colour the world and make it all black
So I am grateful, so grateful that I have friends who get me, who love me,
who are always there for me they take me out of the dark and dismal place make me sparkle and shine
I love those friends of mine

Barbara Soehner

Dear Friends

I still pray for success. Mr. Cancer, I won't let you win. A Dr. recently told me that the type of cancer I suffered is very rare and has very little study done about it. But they do know that it has a high probability of returning within 5 years.
Now they are recommending I keep the port in for all those coming years.
Yes the memories of this past year came back and along with the needles and pin feet. I just sank to a low place and out came the poem posted below. I am so scared. Thank God for my friends in the Instagram community.

Well Hello, Mr. Cancer

My Truth

I never got up today
just stayed in my bed
in a safe place in my head

I never got up today
what does it matter
My truth is this

Round and around I go
My merry go round of woes
My story is a sad one
because I am sick
I have no idea

IF

Barbara Soehner

I will get better
It just hit me today
I realized my truth is this

I never got up today
I didn't eat
I didn't drink
Just stared at the ceiling
The fan spun away
Cooling the air

Thoughts

OK, so this is what I've been doing. I've shut myself inside my body and I'm trapped but I'm safe here. I'm scared but no one can hurt me here.

I went for the CAT scan Saturday and I haven't heard yet. I'm scared that I have cancer again. I probably don't, but it's just hard waiting, so when I heard the poem the other day, I decided to touch on the delirium subject. I went into all the notes on my Mount Sinai chart and it shocked me to read a lot of the notes that different care providers said about me. I had no idea that I was so lost but I guess I was lost for about

Barbara Soehner

I don't know five days maybe.
Anyway, I'm back now and I
love all of you so much and I'm
not much of a poet right

Now I just wanted to make a
statement about what's going
on because I really seem
frozen in time right now.
Love all of you and thank you
for being there always

In honor of Caroline's prompt

My Hair

All of my life I complained about my hair. It was too fine, not pretty like everyone else's and then I started coloring it. I liked it so much and I did highlights in my hair. It truly became a crown I loved. Then all of a sudden Mr Cancer appeared. I was offered the generosity of the Kool Cap. Sadly it didn't help because my hair fell out.

Barbara Soehner

Now I just have a bunch of crumpled grey hair on top of my head and I do not let anybody see it. It remains hidden. My hair is gone

Well Hello, Mr. Cancer

Dear Friends

And so here I am trying to be me again. It's hard, you know, for it's been so long since I've ventured out of my closed self. Been so long since I reached out to people who I know love me. I will try, I will try so hard because I am lonely just being me and I want to belong again to all of you. I want to be part of your lovely world so wish me luck. OK, just wish me luck.

Barbara Soehner

Kind Love

Starting to feel like me again, imagine that!!!
I didn't think I ever would
But I came back
I came back from the ugly evil world
Of liars and cheats and people that aren't nice
As soon as I heard all of your voices here on Instagram, I knew I was safe again.
Thank you for being who you all are.
It means a lot to me.
I love you all so much for we are a family and families are so very special.
No one can destroy kind love

Well Hello, Mr. Cancer

My Mother, Faith made this Angel in her ceramics class. It is so precious to me.

About the Author,
Barbara Soehner
May 5th, 1945 I was born in the sixth month of my gestation at Brooklyn Jewish Hospital in Brooklyn, New York - all 2 pounds of me! They didn't think I would make it but Bravo, I survived.
I grew up in Long Island, New York. I met death for the first time when I was 41 days short of three, as tragically, my mother Marie died when she was only 21 years old. My father remarried and that marriage brought forth 3 brothers and one sister. Life moved on. At 18 I went away to junior college in Washington D.C. I majored in Speech, Drama, Radio and TV. After I graduated,

Well Hello, Mr. Cancer

I landed an agent and earned my living acting in commercials and voice overs for the next 21 years. I started playing guitar and found my true love, songwriting. My wonderful manager Jerry Love, who was the head of A&M records on the east coast, introduced me to a talented songwriting partner Michael Zager. Jerry then left A&M records and they started Love-Zager Music productions.
That is when my creative writing truly began. I wrote with many prolific writers and performed in many clubs, including Reno Sweeney, Tramps & The Grand Finale. One night our guitar player was ill, so my musical director Barbara Morr

Barbara Soehner

hired a brilliant studio guitar player, Jeff Layton. He stepped in without any rehearsals and the show went on.
I married Jeff in 1979. Death came around to visit close to home again. I had five late miscarriages, and two stillbirths. The stillbirth occurred at 21 and 29 weeks. They were both little girls. Then miraculously, we adopted a little boy. He was 36 hours old, and we were truly blessed.
I am so proud of my recent book and audiobook, The Glittering Bird REBORN. It is truly a dream that has come true. I love writing and I am so grateful I found my way.

FIND MORE OF BARBARA SOEHNER HERE!!

Web: www.glitteringbird.com

Amazon; amazon.com/author/barbara soehner

You Tube: Barbara Soehner- The Glittering Bird

Instagram:@barbara_soehner

Facebook: Barbara Soehner/Glitteringbird

SoundCloud: Barbara Soehner

About the Editor

Valerie Lorraine is an author of poetry. She has 2 published books of her poetry collections, and an anthology that includes a heathy body of work from a total of 12 beautiful Poets. She continues to work on more books which include both her own work & more anthologies.

Valerie works as an Editor, Writing Coach and Self Publishing Consultant. Her goal is to direct & encourage those who desire to create a legacy with their pen & their heart. She helps them bring the vision of their art to life.

As an advocate, Valerie gently offers her message. She encourages strength & self love for survivors of domestic violence & emotional trauma.

It is a message she wishes she didn't understand, but is well aware it helped create the person she is proud of today. Valerie is extremely active as a host & mentor.

To find out more, Valerie Lorraine can be found on Instagram @valerielorraineproductions

Books by Valerie can be found on Amazon at amazon.com/author/valerie_lorraine